I0159669

A Loss for Words

Remembering animals loved and lost

Myrna Milani, DVM

©Myrna Milani, 2011

All rights reserved. No part of this book may be reproduced or transmitted in any form or by any means, electronic or mechanical, including photocopying, recording, or by any information storage or retrieval system, without permission from the author, except for the inclusion of quotations in a review.

Published by Fainshaw Press, Charlestown, New Hampshire

ISBN: 978 943290126

DEDICATION

This book is dedicated to all of the clients, friends and family who have shared their stories of animals loved and lost. Now it's my turn to reciprocate.

Table of Contents

Table of Contents

ACKNOWLEDGMENTS

I'd like to acknowledge the hard work and unstinting technical and emotional support from Carole Stein and Jeremy and Daniel Milani. Without them this book and *The Veterinarian's Guide to Pet* Loss would not have been possible.

Introduction

When I was a teenager, I read a lot of science fiction/fantasy, particularly short stories. One that made a particularly strong impression on me concerned a man who witnessed a seemingly endless stream of horrible accidents involving all kinds of vehicles. As the never-ending sequence of mayhem and destruction continued, I shared the main character's desire for an end to the misery. It finally arrived on the last page when he awoke exhausted on a bed in a small room. Shortly thereafter a disembodied voice asked him, "How many?" and he answered "1287." In the next and final paragraph of the story, the reason for this insanity became clear. Someone in a city far away turned on the evening news and heard a newscaster announce, "The National Road Safety Alliance estimates that 1287 people will die in traffic accidents this holiday weekend. Please drive carefully."

I remembered that story less than a decade later when, as a young female veterinarian in what was then a heavily male-dominated profession, I inherited the bulk of the euthanasias in the busy practice where I worked. Initially I bought into the idea that this provided me with a fail-safe way to learn the basics of intravenous injections and client communication. That delusion vanished by the end of the first week when I realized what my employers already knew: without exception, a properly done euthanasia ranks as the most challenging procedure in the veterinary repertoire for those whose training is deeply entrenched in the preservation of life. Attend an animal's death in the owner's presence and we're talking veterinary Olympics.

I admit that I, cloaked in my new life-saving degree as I was, initially resented getting plunged into this deepest, darkest end of the practice pool so unceremoniously. But I also could understand my employers' desire to spare themselves of at least some of this responsibility after bearing it for so many years. Even so, there was a period during which I feared that I'd fall asleep and dream of every animal whose death I'd attended every night for the rest of my life. Not only the litters of unwanted puppies and kittens that were still fairly common in New England back then, but all of the animals who succumbed to life-threatening injuries or illnesses, too.

Nor did attending the death of all those animals become easier, any more than doing so made it any easier to deal with the loss of my own. True, I knew the mechanics of the process better than most and felt far more comfortable in the clinic surroundings than the average client. But minus those two concerns, I had more energy to devote to the denial, anger, bargaining, depression, and acceptance sequence that almost inevitably accompanies the loss of an animal to one degree or another. And at each stage, my knowledge of animal health, behavior, and the human-animal bond enabled me to throw up additional barriers as I made my way toward acceptance.

But inevitably, I did reach it.

Sweet, blessed acceptance. Following the deaths of Whittington, BeeBee, and Violet described in the pages ahead, my one desire was to get out of the clinic and, hopefully, home before I lost it. Aside from a few tears, I always made it at least to the car. After that it was iffy, but the roads between the clinic and my home aren't that heavily traveled. Even if people who passed me saw the tears, they didn't see the dead animal wrapped in a towel or blanket on the passenger seat beside me. Or my right hand stroking the head protruding from the swaddled bundle. For me it was during this unlikely interval that the healing began.

Sometimes the acceptance came swiftly, marked by the planting of a particular flower on a grave. Other times it crept up on me. One cat who disappeared showed up in my dreams for several years, the only one of my animals I can remember dreaming about. I noticed that she no longer did about the same time that I noticed I'd stopped looking along the side of the road for evidence of her, dead or alive. Were the two events related? I have no idea, but choose to see her presence in my dreams until I accepted her loss as another of those inexplicable final animal gifts.

Years ago I would have marked the passing of well-loved animals in letters to a few close friends. They would have phoned or sent a letter or card of condolence in response and that would be it. Over time, I'd forget what I'd written and they'd forget what they read.

Not that this is necessarily a bad way to do things. Hanging on to those final moments too long makes it more difficult to keep the memory of the good times alive. Still, there's something to be said for the electronic age that allows us to mark such passing in commentaries on websites, blogs, podcasts, and other forms of online memorials. Rereading and in one case listening to my thoughts about these events brought the animals and the lives we shared very much to life again, even the fictional one. It also made me recognize their continued beneficial impact on the life I share with all animals now.

Because of this, I agree with Albert Schweitzer's Reverence for Life philosophy. Not the interpretation advocated by those who choose to perceive all animal death as wrong. But rather as he proposed it: that no death should go unnoticed. In other words, we owe all living beings a mindful death.

But mindful death isn't easy. It takes courage to know when to let go of the animal and more to actually do it. Sometimes more courage than I thought I had. It takes faith in the relationship to let go of the grief and remember the good times instead. Sometimes more faith than I thought I had. It takes love that exceeds any fears. Sometimes more love than I thought I had, too. And it takes acceptance that life is finite which, oddly enough, has become easier as I've gotten older.

Perhaps because I've shared my life with such grand animal teachers.

Still, it's not an easy process. In the short run, it hurts. Sometimes it hurts like hell.

But surviving it leads to a final paradox, the joy of loss. Had there not been a Whittington, BeeBee, Violet the WonderDog and all their predecessors loved and lost, it would have taken me a lot longer to learn that reverence for life does indeed grow out of the acceptance of every loss. Had it not been for all those animals loved and lost—not only my own but also those belonging to others—I wouldn't cherish my animals, the natural world, and life itself as much as I do now. Had I not experienced this elegant cycle countless times over the years, I would not have realized that this is the way it's meant to be.

For this final gift from each and every one of them, I remain forever grateful.

Myrna Milani, DVM

Charlestown, NH

A Tribute to Whittington the Cat

This essay originally appeared as a commentary on my website and represented yet another chapter in my on-going quest for making the inevitable loss of a long-time animal companion easier to bear. It did, but the actual event couldn't go unnoticed either

Years ago I heard an interview with author Ray Bradbury in which he extolled the value of fan letters. He wasn't just referring to the letters that his own fans had written to him that had given him great joy, but also to those letters he himself had written to those from all walks of life. I still recall his passionate message: Don't put it off. Do it now. Tell them before they die how much you admire them.

Not too long ago, it hit me that my cat Whittington is going to be 14 this spring, a thought that elicited all those death-related concerns, and with them the certainty that I would write a tribute to him when he died. But then I remembered what Bradbury had said. Why wait until Whittington dies to pay tribute to him? Why not write a fan letter to him right now?

And so I did.

Whittington the Cat was born the end of March, beginning of April under a porch in 1994. By today's standards that would have made him feral, but he'd have none of that. He knew he wasn't feral any more than his mother was. There's no shame in being born on the wrong side of the porch as it were. No need to deny his mother was a stray.

Far too soon Whittington was separated from his mom and put up for adoption. Sure, he was big enough to eat kitten food, but he still needed her comfort. Luckily for him, he came into my life about the same time as Watson the Hound who allowed Whit to suck on his ear or head when life overwhelmed him. Had he not chosen Watson and had Watson not so graciously accepted the role of surrogate mom, I would have given him a toy or blanket to suck instead. (Fortunately by then I knew that animals suck for comfort as well as nourishment and that the timeframe of the latter may be much longer than the former.) I would lie in bed at night and hear the sucking sounds coming from the dog bed on the floor beside mine, then the purrs, then the soft sounds of feline sleep as Whit drifted off contentedly.

Perhaps because Watson allowed him to do this, from the beginning Whit had a very special relationship with the dog. That Watson permitted him to nurse not surprisingly led to the logical feline conclusion that Watson was his surrogate mom. Alas, Watson had the habit of engaging in some distinctly unfeline activities that disrupted this illusion. The worst of these was that, unlike a well-bred cat like Whittington, Watson did not dig a hole, eliminate in it, and neatly cover it when he finished.

I still clearly recall the look of horror that crossed Whit's face the first time he happened to be nearby when the dog just, God forbid, took a dump and walked away. It was winter and at first Whit just stood there, looking from Watson to the pile of poo and back again as if trying to will the dog to rectify this gross oversight. When Watson wandered off to do other doggy things Whit set about covering the pile with snow, just as a child might cover a faux pas committed by a beloved adult.

Fortunately Whittington is very smart and was able to figure out most of the early cat lessons he'd missed on his own. Aside from the little quirks introduced into his behavior by his relationship with Watson, he was completely and unapologetically a cat. Just as he shrugged off definitions of himself as feral, he also found the idea that some considered domestic cats a social species relative to their own kind laughable. As soon as he hit maturity, he had no use for any cat in his yard or his house. Although he's a small cat, he's always been a very big feline presence.

Nor did Whittington ever rush to greet visitors to my home like some dog. His immediate response was to disappear. But this was always by choice, not out of fear, something he proved conclusively on two occasions. The first occurred when a crew was filming a segment on feline behavior here at the house. I'd recruited a couple more social cats because I knew Whit wouldn't cooperate and the crew was well aware of this. As they were packing up their equipment after we finished, several commented on their desire to see the ephemeral resident cat. Sure enough and as if on cue, as soon as they were all loaded up and beginning to back their vehicle out of its parking space, Whit appeared and sat on the front step and groomed himself as if he'd been there all the time.

The second instance requires that I set the scene. I live in a very old house and I've discovered that some people do not like very old houses because of their real or imaginary strange noises. There are times when Whittington sleeps in a floor-to-ceiling cupboard in the bathroom that has one of those louvered doors that looks like it consists of two smaller doors that open from the middle, but there's actually a hinge in the middle. Because of this, Whit can open it by hooking a front paw under the bottom of the door near the hinge, and pulling. Once he does, he jumps onto the bottom shelf and curls up to sleep in the corner on an old fleece shirt of mine.

Sometimes when I expect company I'll notice that the door

is slightly open and automatically shut it, forgetting that he might be sleeping in there. On several occasions, Whit has waited until someone has come into the bathroom to use the facilities, then slowly opened the door from the inside. So far the answer to the question "Who is more shocked, women or men?" is that it's pretty much a draw. Women who have watched the door slowly open while they were sitting on the john seem as stunned as men who were standing peeing with their back to said closet when they heard the door began to open. In all cases, once Whit opened the cupboard, he then appeared and calmly walked to the bathroom door and politely waited to be let out.

Perhaps the reason Whittington is so unabashedly solitary and territorial, i.e. so quintessentially country cat, is because he's also such a skilled predator. Hunting is not a team endeavor for small cats. It requires a tremendous amount of knowledge, patience and self-control. One mistake and it can cost a cat a meal or even his life.

For those who live in more refined environments, the predatory cat is an embarrassment, a violation of the Peaceable Kingdom mystique. But the core of my house was built in the 1700s and one mortarless stone wall in the basement is literally at one with the earth. I have had water snakes glide over my feet while I was moving laundry from the washer to the dryer. I have liberated I don't know how many rodents from the recycling containers near the wall. (Once I somehow missed a rat in one of them—until he ran over my feet when I was driving to the dump!) Were it not for Whit, I would have to use chemicals to kill these critters because otherwise nothing in my house on that large menu of rodent edibles would be safe. As it is, they and he have established a workable balance. They can live and raise their families within the shelter of the crawl space under the living room, but if they dare venture into the house itself, they will regret it. Unless, of course, I happen to be around.

Even though I do appreciate Whit's hunting skills, I have been known to interrupt a hunt because... I really don't know why. When I interrupt, he looks at me the same way he and his

12

predecessor looked at the succession of pups they tried unsuccessfully to teach to hunt: with an expression of scorn tinged with pity, as if to say, "You still don't get it, do you?" I'd like to claim some higher moral ground here, but I'm not that naive. I know he's coming from a place that my limited human perception and thought processes, and perhaps even their resultant limited sense of morality, cannot take me.

Whittington also considers dogs the greatest cat toys ever invented. He uses his tail like a lure to entice the younger dogs to get close to his hiding place under the couch or behind the shower curtain. When they inevitably do, he spins and smacks them with his paws then takes off with them in hot pursuit. The games he plays with deaf, visually impaired BeeBee would hardly win any political correctness awards because he mercilessly capitalizes on her limitations. But she doesn't seem to mind in the least when he sneaks up and bats her from behind because she didn't see him sneak out from the far end of the couch like the other dogs did. When he smacks her, she's more than happy to shriek in delight and chase him in her unique uncoordinated, bouncy way.

One would think that this glowing tribute would include something about Whit's unfailing presence on my bed every night, his instinctive awareness of when I'm feeling down and in need an encouraging head butt or purr, but such is not the case. Maybe he thinks I get enough of such fawning from the dogs. Maybe he thinks I should trust the love and not need such evidence. Maybe he thinks that, if I don't trust it, I should learn.

From the beginning and through more than a decade, above all, always a cat.

Addendum: Whit and I made his final journey almost a year after I wrote the above, I recorded this podcast the next day, and felt better after I did.
http://blog.mmilani.com/504/meandering-with-myrn-28/

A LOSS FOR WORDS

The Death of Sneakers

Sneakers lived and died in one of a series of unpublished animal behavior and bond-related mysteries I wrote that feature veterinarian StClair Upton and her sometimes partner, Chandler McCarthy. The plot of this one revolves around elderly Herbert Dodge, an introverted New Hampshire farmer who lives at Meadowridge Farm with his timid miniature poodle. In addition to sharing similar temperaments, dog and owner are both overweight and suffer from heart problems. In human-animal bond jargon, the two are medically and behaviorally co-dependent. In this scene, Herb has collapsed and in the confusion to rush him to the hospital, nobody thinks about the dog and how much she means to him and vice versa. Except StClair. As she drives to the farm to search for the dog, she alerts Herb's veterinarian, Tony Minnini.

As I drove McCarthy's car to Herb's, I did something I vowed I'd never do: I used the phone he'd left in the vehicle. For many reasons—some of them logical, most of them not—I felt the quality of life took a giant step backward with the invention of the cell phone, let alone all the portable electronic paraphernalia that followed it. Even so I was grateful I could call Tony and put him on stand-by alert. Just in case.

Just in case what I didn't want to know.

When I opened the door of the old farmhouse, my heart sank when I saw the kitchen table shoved against one wall and its chairs shoved haphazardly against the others. I could easily imagine the self-styled doc-jock paramedics descending on Meadowridge, hellbent on saving a life as dramatically as possible. What I couldn't imagine was them taking the time to notice a terrified old dog.

I was wrong. After fruitlessly searching the house for over an hour, I finally found Sneakers lying comatose in a little used pantry where someone evidently had put her to get her out of the way.

"It's going to be all right," I murmured, a sentiment I didn't really believe as I gave her a cursory examination.

As if knowing my thoughts, she stopped breathing and her heart stopped beating. Without giving it a second thought, I extended her neck, covered her mouth and nose with my lips, exhaled twice into her, then cupped her chest between my hands and compressed it rhythmically. When I began the fourth sequence of breaths and compressions, I felt a faint flutter beneath my hands and my own heart pounded with hope. By the time I breathed into the dog again fifteen seconds later, I could feel a heartbeat.

Not a good one, but it was there.

And then a breath.

And then another.

Sneakers continued to breathe until I reached Tony's hospital, but then her old heart stopped again. I grabbed the fat little bundle and raced into the treatment room where Tony immediately took her and placed her on a stainless steel table.

That single act initiated a precise chain of events that I watched from the sidelines, knowing I would only be in the way if I tried to help. A technician inserted an endotracheal tube and began ventilating Sneakers, complimenting the pace of Tony's compression of the old dog's chest. Another colleague inserted an IV catheter, while a third wrapped Sneakers' hind legs and posterior abdomen with elastic bandages to increase her blood pressure and maintain the flow to her vital organs. The associate who applied the bandages then placed her hand over Sneakers' anterior abdomen to help maintain the pressure in her chest and the flow of blood to her brain. Someone else kept advancing the drugs and equipment in the cardiopulmonary resuscitation tray so whatever was needed for the next step always stood ready. Everything that Tony could possibly do, he did.

When Sneakers' heart still didn't beat, Tony changed his position and the position of his hands on her chest. When it still didn't beat, he compressed her chest faster and then slower, with more and with less force. And each time everyone on the team followed the sequence.

A hundred twenty times a minute.

He injected epinephrine, the most powerful of the drugs used in resuscitation and compressed the tiny chest again.

Still Sneakers' heart didn't beat. I ticked off the devastating, but pathetically small passages of significant time. Tony never took his eyes off the dog, but precisely five minutes after he began resuscitating her, he picked up a pair of clippers and quickly shaved the area between her fifth and sixth ribs. He swabbed it once with an antiseptic solution and picked up a scalpel.

At this point he should have incised the skin and tissue down to the cellophane thin lining of her chest cavity. Then he should have penetrated the lining with his finger or a hemostat, then extended the incision. And then he should have held the poodle's tiny heart between his thumb and index finger and compressed it rhythmically.

I saw him doing all these things the instant he picked up the scalpel. I saw the worn-out old heart between his gentle but

17

sure fingers. I could even feel the warm, thin, overly stretched cardiac muscle, smell the almost sweet, moist scent of barely living tissue.

But Tony didn't actually do any of those things. He brought the blade down to within a hair's breadth of Sneakers' skin then turned to me with the unasked question in his eyes.

In that instant whatever seductive hold the technology and fear of death held over me vanished.

I shook my head.

For another minute nobody moved. And then as miraculously as it had appeared, all the equipment vanished, followed a short time later by everyone except Tony and me.

Eight minutes and thirty seconds after they ran into the room.

It seemed like a lifetime.

For Sneakers it was.

***

I patted the little dog's head one last time and tried unsuccessfully to convey my gratitude to Tony. He shooed me out a side door where I found myself standing next to McCarthy's car unable to comprehend the strange noises coming from it. Eventually it dawned on me that it was his phone emitting an anemic version of the William Tell Overture.

"Are you all right?" The sound of relief in McCarthy's voice filled the dull day with instant light.

"Do you realize how many times we use the greeting 'Are you all right' lately?" I sighed tiredly. "Why can't we lead a normal life where you call to remind me to bring home a quart of milk instead of to check if I'm dead or not?"

"Beats me. I assume you're not dead?"

"No, I'm not, but Sneakers is." My voice broke and he wisely said nothing for the next few minutes.

After I assured him that I was fine, I hung up and drove to the campus then walked to the Hanover Clinic in the rain. No sooner did I enter the third floor waiting room that served the intensive care unit than a very haggard Daphne Zimmerman rushed to greet me. When I learned she had been sitting there for over five hours without a word about Herb from anyone on the staff, I decided to take action.

After dismissing Daphne to go home and get some rest and leaving a message for McCarthy telling him I intended to stay with Herb, I located his room. Slowly I walked toward the observation window that separated the unit's empty nurse's station from it and stared through the glass open-mouthed. Everywhere I looked I saw medical stuff, more stuff than I thought could find a place on the human body to pump, measure, add fluids, remove them, shock, or otherwise manipulate it to keep it going. And in the midst of it all lay Herb Dodge who we all considered far too fat for his own good, looking like a deflated balloon. I leaned my head against the coolness of the glass, closed my eyes, and wished I were dead like Sneakers.

The sudden appearance of a firm hand on the back of my neck made me think I might get my wish. But instead of mounting some great McCarthyesque counter-attack, I jumped and screamed so feebly that I wouldn't have deterred a geriatric mouse, let alone that as yet unknown human determined to eliminate anyone who got in his way.

"Did I scare you?" McCarthy's question immediately reminded me that this was the day I'd designated him the Great Nonverbal Communicator what now seemed like ages ago.

"You think spending the night here's a good idea, Clair?" he continued before I could answer.

I nodded affirmatively.

"I want to be here when he wakes up to tell him about Sneakers."

"What if he doesn't ask?"

"Then I suggest you check outside for flying elephants," I smiled sadly. "Believe me, he'll ask."

McCarthy left and about an hour later a nurse came in, made a few inconsequential comments, did nursing things, then disappeared—a sure sign that Herb's pain-in-the-behind enfant terrible cardiologist was willing to tolerate my presence. An hour after that, Herb awoke.

19

He looked at me.

I looked at him.

And he knew.

The two of us clung to each other and cried for the little dog. For a brief instant I wondered if it was good for him to be sobbing like that, but the moment past. Surely it would be a hundred times worse for him if he couldn't grieve.

And grieve we did. I told him what I did, what Tony and his staff did, and when I told Tony to quit and why. Finally we reminisced quietly about Sneakers for a long time and even managed a smile or two. And then Herb fell asleep.

***

The next day McCarthy met me with one of his interminable do-lists and a look of determination in his eyes as I was leaving the hospital. Before he could say a word, I announced with equal determination, "I'm not doing anything until I bury Sneakers."

He stopped dead and because he had his arm around me, I naturally stopped with him.

"I promised Herb I'd do it," I explained when he continued looking at me oddly.

"Please?" I finished lamely, suddenly fearing he wouldn't let me perform this final task first.

"Of course, you can do it," he finally answered and hugged me for some some reason I couldn't fathom.

Later when I dug the hole among the daffodils, lined it with pine boughs, and laid the curly-coated little cinder block's remains to rest in accord with Herb's wishes, I caught McCarthy watching me through the window. When I captured and held his deep blue gaze, I didn't see the familiar, slightly bewildered but patient tolerance he usually expressed when I fulfilled an obligation related to my work with animals that was so remote from his own experience. Instead, I saw a sadness every bit as profound as my own.

But more than that I saw the awe of a person discovering for the first time that he, too, could care so very much about the death of a pathetic old dog he barely knew.

20

Digging BeeBee's Grave

If ever a dog existed with symbolic potential, BeeBee was the one. The offspring of champion Pembroke Welsh corgis, her multiple mind-body defects could fuel all kinds of speculations spanning the spectrum from expected results of a pathologically restricted gene pool to acts of God. In addition to all that those defects did to her, they made her one of the greatest teaching animals I ever knew.

When I taught a bioethics course at the local community college one of the units the students and I explored was the loss of young versus geriatric individuals. A quote from a father whose 10-year-old son died of cancer remains with me: "He live more in his 10 years than many will live in a lifetime."

So it was with BeeBee. The following two blogs marked the end of a lifetime condensed into our quixotic two years together.

I was thinking about my dad when I was digging BeeBee's grave. He was a great nature lover, but the last person you'd want around if you found a chipmunk mangled by a cat or a bird with a broken wing. He'd get so overwhelmed by emotion that the animal would pass from critical condition to beyond hope before the objective part of his brain started to work again.

Because the two of us were so much alike in many ways, I had to practice long and hard as a veterinary student not to let my emotions get the best of me, too. It wasn't easy, but most of the time I managed to hold it together long enough to objectively analyze what was going on, how best to address it, and get the job done. Only after it was over would I allow myself to break down.

It hasn't worked that way with Bee. I vowed I'd make a list of all of her existing and potential problems before I called a friend who's a shelter director about finding a new home for her, and I did. But with each new addition, I realized that the probability of finding someone willing and able to do all I've done to give Bee the semblance of a normal life these past two years was about nil. That made me cry. The probability of finding someone who could detect, let alone correctly interpret, her unique body language lexicon to pick up subtle signs of change was even less likely. That made me cry even more. Until I made the list, I didn't realize that creating a semblance of a normal Beebee had required more than 35 years of veterinary and ethological knowledge and a semi-solitary lifestyle in an environment that was, for the most part, amazingly well-suited to the special needs of a deaf, visually impaired, brain-damaged dog with multiple physical problems, any one of which could blow up at any moment. The awareness that even that wasn't enough made me cry harder still.

I knew that reaching adulthood would be Bee's Rubicon. The fact that she apparently believed herself to be a 100% mentally and physically normal corgi had served us well when she was younger. It resulted in an indefatigable joie de vivre and can-do spirit worthy of a Marine recruiting poster. Although I don't think she realized it (or cared if she did), her mind enabled her body to be much, much more than it should have been.

But when Bee reached two, that same mind worked against her because it told her that 5-year-old Frica should cede rank to her. From the beginning the other animals have been aware of Bee's limitations and have learned to read her foreign body language and tolerate her rough play and the occasionally accidental, but nonetheless painful, encounter with the teeth in her grossly misshapen jaw. But Fric ceding her job to Bee would be like Hilary Clinton ceding hers to Helen Keller. To the normal canine mind, there was no reason to do this.

BeeBee couldn't accept that. Her attempts to signal rank over Fric became more intense and unpredictable with that wonky jaw of hers being the ever-present potentially lethal wild card. This week she launched a sneak attack on Fric and attempted to grab her by the muzzle. This time one of her wayward fangs slammed into Fric's lower jaw and bent her incisors sufficiently that they had to be removed. Given Bee's intensity and that she weighs twice as much as Frica, it was a miracle that Fric's jaw wasn't broken.

At that point I knew that Bee had crossed the Rubicon, determined to assume what would have been her rightful place had her body been as normal as her mind. But it's not and the result is taking its toll on all of us, a toll that can only get higher in the days ahead. While the little dogs and the cat stay out of Bee's way, she increasing alarm-barks and charges at something none of the other animals acknowledge as real. The celebratory zoomies that used to have all three dogs racing around the house or yard playing tag have been replaced by intense, short charges back and forth as if she's not sure what she wants, to play or attack. Because of her increasingly unusual signals, none of the animals want anything to do with her and that frustrates her even more.

By the time I finished the list, I knew that the only answer was euthanasia. I couldn't bear the thought of someone with rescue-itis taking her, convinced that how good she looked couldn't take that much time and effort for someone with a lot of love to give. I didn't want her to go to some well-meaning but naive person like my dad, only to have her or someone else get hurt because they let their guard down for just a minute, or because they just couldn't believe that such a sweet dog wouldn't like their Aunt Harriet's peek-a-poo.

No. Far better Bee and I should make that final journey together later this morning and that I somehow manage, once again, to hold it together long enough to see her on her way to what I hope is better place.

For all that I observed and interacted with Bee during our relatively short but transformative time together, I never was able to grasp what her reality was no matter how hard I tried. At most, all I had were glimpses of it. She taught me that sometimes words are useless and that hand signals aren't much better. And during those special times when we connected on a level I'd never connected with an animal before, I realized she made me a lot more than I ever thought I'd be, too.

After I bury Bee, I'm planting a large pulmonaria from another part of the garden over her grave. Maybe this fall, but definitely by next spring it will produce flowers that are half blue and half pink, a fitting tribute to a dog who tried so hard to live in two different worlds at once, but ultimately couldn't.

BeeBee: The Day After

I didn't manage the tear-control I'd hoped for when I participated in BeeBee's euthanasia yesterday, but I survived. It was pouring rain and the drive to the clinic was miserable with traffic slowed to a crawl where portions of the road were covered with water. Bee didn't like rain under the best of circumstances and these were anything but.

As soon as I got home, I buried her with a favorite toy and the tags from her collar, then planted the Pulmonaria on top of her amid a cairn of large rocks to deter curious critters. I knew the body would decay and nourish the plants around her over time, and soon their botanical transpiration (i.e., respiration) would cause them to give off oxygen that I, the other pets, and all beings in our environment would inhale, making her immortal in a way as well as part of us all.

But those metal tags and her skeleton will last a lot longer. And if at some point far in the future someone happened to dig in the area, I like to think they would look at her bones and those tags the same way today's archeologists look at certain ancient canine or feline remains and say, "This wasn't some stray or feral animal who died here. This animal belonged to someone who cared."

As a veterinarian first in medical practice and now in a behavioral/bond one who also has shared her life with a lot of animals, I've done a lot of grieving in my life. But each time it's different. Regardless what others may choose to believe, I didn't put Bee down for just behavioral problems, if for no other reason than that such don't exist. I am completely aware of all the physiological and bond (both human and that with with members of other species) components of behavioral problems, more so than I've ever been in my life. Because of all of Bee's hereditary and congenital problems, I had to know more about and be more aware of this interaction 24 hours a day, day in and day out than with any other being of any species with whom I've ever lived. Because of this, I knew professionally, scientifically, and intuitively what most people only know intuitively: that it was time to let her go.

Because of that, I'm free of any guilt and doubt—my own or that which others would try to impose on me. I'm free to experience the loss of Bee as a loss of Bee, and not the the loss of a symbol of someone or something else I may not even consciously acknowledge as real. I don't feel obligated to feel repulsed because my other animals are visibly more relaxed and playful, although sometimes as confused as I am by all the changes in our routine. Ollie still waits at the top of the stairs for me to pick up Bee and descend first, and I still stop to do just that. I make twice as many trips up and down the stairs as I now need to, once to transport any books, cups of tea, cleaning supplies or other paraphernalia, and a second to transport a dog incapable of climbing stairs who's no longer there.

Even though I intellectually and intuitively recognized the inextricable relationship between health, behavior, and the bond, Bee's many problems never permitted me of the luxury of denying this as is often possible with other animals. Whether I wanted to or not, I had to be aware of it because her life depended on it. But in the process of doing this, I learned to communicate in a way I'd never experienced with an animal before.

Bee couldn't hear, her vision was impaired in ways I could never define to my satisfaction, she responded defensively to all but a narrow range of touch, her sense of smell was incredible, but only sometimes. Sometimes she was quite

26

solidly here, but other times she was somewhere else. In short, the kinds of sensory perception that form the foundation of normal human-companion animal communication were unreliable or nonexistent. So we came up with something new. Not some special form made up for my own convenience that I taught her using treats as I would have done years ago. This time I summoned the patience and dumped enough of my considerable human ego to let her teach me.

Now I look at the other dogs and know it's time to play catch-up. Aside from the basic training I didn't have time for— all I cared about was a reliable response to the come command—I want to rethink my ideas of quality interspecies communication with them as well as the cat. Because of Bee, I stopped being so verbal with them months ago and didn't rely nearly as much on visual cues, either. But because they were so stable and reliably good, I never had to develop that—what? transcendent?—plane of communication with them that I did with Bee.

I still don't have to. But now and thanks to BeeBee, I want to.

A LOSS FOR WORDS

MYRNA MILANI, DVM

A LOSS FOR WORDS

Violet The WonderDog

Violet was also a Pembroke Welch corgi and about as opposite from Bee as imaginable. Where Bee could claim high-class credentials, Violet's birth resulted from an illicit coupling of two adults with immune issues, specifically a predilection for producing offspring prone to demodectic mange. Whereas I got BeeBee when the breeder gave her up to a shelter, I scoped out Violet's litter in the cluttered but clean modular home she shared with her parents, littermates, the breeder and her kids. Ironically given her lowly beginnings, Violet was such a physically and behaviorally sound dog, I swore I'd never get another corgi because none could possibly live up to her standard. Nor did I until several years later when fate brought BeeBee into my life. But Bee dwelt in her own world so remote from Violet's that comparing them never occurred to me. On the other hand, BeeBee and I undoubtedly benefitted from all I learned from Vi.

On Friday June 25, 2004, Violet the WonderDog and my almost constant companion for more than 14 years, died peacefully in my arms following euthanasia. And although I'm tempted to go on and on about her in an effort to vanquish the pain of loss more quickly, it seems more in keeping with who and what she was to share less weepy thoughts that occurred following her death. More specifically, thoughts elicited by two quite different sources: the Summer 2004 edition of the Dartmouth Medicine newsletter and *The Old American*, a novel by Ernest Hebert (Hardscrabble Press).

Like many owners of aging well-loved pets, during my last month with Violet all the questions associated with euthanasia would creep into my thoughts no matter how hard I tried to keep them out. In spite of the fact that I intellectually knew that the nature of the bond we shared guaranteed that, when the time came to let her go, I would know it and respond in the right way (not too early, not too late), I could never get rid of that last, nagging tinge of doubt no matter how hard I tried.

That Friday morning when it was so obvious that the time had come based on the unspoken pact that she and I had made years ago, I nonetheless reverted to my scientific training. She'd eaten some that morning and that was good, even though I had to hand-feed her for the first time in her life and it seemed like she took the food more to please me than because she was hungry. Sure, she lost control of her bladder and was getting progressively weaker in the rear end, but a lot of things could cause that. Ditto for her increasingly frequent bouts of labored breathing. As I sat there, I clinically rattled off a list of all the tests I'd ask the vets at the clinic to run when I took her in.

And then I looked at her as someone she trusted rather than as a fearful owner or science-blinded clinician. In that instant, I knew that this was not what I was going to ask them to do. This could be total projection on my part, but it seemed to me that I saw Vi heave a sigh of relief when I acknowledged this. For the first time in her life, rather than waiting for me to invite her to go somewhere with me, she went and lay quietly by the door. For the first time in her life, she told me it was time to go.

The article in Dartmouth Medicine was entitled "Striking variations revealed in end-of-life care at 'best hospitals'." By studying the records of the 77 hospitals listed in U.S. News and Business Report's 2001 'America's Best Hospitals' issue, a team of researchers headed by Dr. John Wennberg discovered "huge differences" in the care those with chronic illnesses received during the last six months of life. In spite of the fact that all of the hospitals studied were academic medical centers with excellent reputations for state-of-the-art care for geriatric patients as well as those suffering from heart and lung diseases and cancer, the treatment of individual patients varied widely.

Aside from the fact that this study indicated that these bastions of medical science had no science-based standard when it came to end-of-life care, it corroborated the findings of previous studies. And those studies revealed that the kinds and duration of services terminal human patients received was more a function of the number of physicians and beds available than the patients' preferences or needs.

As I read this, I thought about Violet's death and the rural Vermont veterinary clinic in which it occurred. The idea that her care and the manner and timing of her death would be determined by the number of empty cages or practitioners was ludicrous. Her death, like her life, reminded me once again of why I chose to be a veterinarian rather than a physician. Veterinary medicine is much more humane, I think. And although I know that some veterinarians aspire to be like the "real doctors," I pray that their desire will never go so far that they deny well-bonded owners the right and privilege to let their suffering animals die quickly, quietly, and with peace and dignity rather than slowly and possibly painfully fading away, separated from their loved ones just to fill a cage.

In The Old American, author Ernie Hebert's main character, Caucus-Meteor, a Native American, states that the period of mourning following the death of a loved one is a function of any guilt and regret one had about the relationship with that other when he/she was alive. The more guilt and

33

regrets, the longer the period of mourning, and the greater the reluctance to engage in another relationship.

People ask me, "Are you going to get another dog?"

Oh, yeah.

Definitely.

MYRNA MILANI, DVM

A LOSS FOR WORDS

A Fond Farewell

From *The Veterinarian's Guide to Pet Loss*

Back in the old days of science, the dour Victorian gurus of animal behavior insisted that only young animals played, and they only played in order to learn how to hunt and mate. But as any observant pet owner knows and as more enlightened scientists later proved, animals of all ages play. While animals do, indeed, use play to learn (because doing so constitutes the most efficient way to do this), they also communicate an entirely different message with these displays. Their playful spirits make it known that, no matter how bad circumstances may appear to others, they not only can cope, they possess enough energy to enjoy themselves, too.

This realization creates a paradox for us humans, however. Logic tells us that, the more we need to learn and the more difficult the situation, the more we also need playfulness and humor to help us, too. But many in our society still apply that same dour Victorian view to humans, saying we can't express joy or playfulness when a beloved animal dies.

"It's at least disrespectful," they warn us ominously. "If not downright crazy."

So what to do?

I say express it anyhow.

I dedicated A Veterinarian's Guide to Pet Loss to an animal-loving friend and former veterinary technician. During the more than three decades our friendship spans, we've loved and lost a mind-boggling number of patients and personal pets of all species under the best and worst of circumstances. I suspect you could build a pyramid sufficient to hold both of our remains out of the empty boxes once filled with the Kleen-X we and our clients used to wipe our tears during that time. At the same time, though, I can't remember a single instance when one or the other of us didn't muster the wherewithal to say or do something that made us both smile.

Maybe in our line of work you do that to keep your sanity. Still, I know of many owners who somehow manage to do the same thing, and I know it springs from their confidence in their ability to cope and, above all, their confidence in the quality of their relationship with the animal. I think one of my clients summed up this particular magic best when he made a comment that caused us both to laugh through our tears after we put his pet to sleep.

"She was such a great friend," he then said. "I just had to say good-bye to her with a smile."

Surely no one could ask for a final tribute greater than that.

If you would like to pay tribute to your beloved pet, I have made arrangements for you to build an online pet memorial webpage and receive a 50% discount. Simply go to: http://www.onlinepetmemorials.com. At checkout, use coupon code: petloss.

The Author

In addition to her clinical practice Myrna Milani has written numerous articles and books, and presented seminars on companion animal behavior and the bond for professionals and the general public. She was the 2009 recipient of the Eli Lilly Lectureship to further knowledge of the physiological, psychological, and sociological of the human-companion animal bond. You can learn more about her and her work at www.mmilani.com.

Other Books by Myrna Milani, DVM

The Veterinarian's Guide to Pet Loss

Preparing for the Loss of Your Pet

The Art of Veterinary Practice

The Weekend Dog

The Invisible Leash

Dog Smart

Cat Smart

The Body Language and Emotion of Dogs

The Body Language and Emotion of Cats

MYRNA MILANI, DVM

www.ingramcontent.com/pod-product-compliance
Lightning Source LLC
Chambersburg PA
CBHW030307030426
42337CB00012B/617